BE A UNICORN

& live life on the bright side

BE A UNICORN

& live life on the bright side

SARAH FORD

ILLUSTRATED BY
ANITA MANGAN

spruce

FOR FLORRIE

NOTES

Always read this book with a smile on your face, but not on the toilet (unicorns would never do that).

Contains explicitly happy content.

Rated PG (good for positivity guidance).

Not for non-believers.

Spread the love.

Be a unicorn. Unicorn is fearless and kind, he always tries to be positive and see the good in others, but he also loves laughter and mischief, so be on guard, as there is often a harmless prank up his sleeve.

Unicorn likes to see the funny side of things and enjoys everything he does.

He is proud to be different and full of positive energy; you will never find Unicorn standing on the sidelines. He is always the first on the dance floor and doesn't care what anyone else thinks... after all music and body are made for enjoyment. Unicorn is happy in his own skin, he loves himself and everyone around him. He chooses to live in the moment and doesn't dwell on the past (that's gone), or worry about the future (who knows what that will bring).

If you live life like Unicorn then you are destined to be happy, with a full cup that overflows with glitter and goodness.

Be a unicorn, and you will make the world a more colourful, happy and peaceful place.

UNICORN'S 10 RULES FOR A GOOD LIFE

- Be nice. It's free and easy, and if you do stuff for others it makes you feel really good inside.

- A little bit of daydreaming can be fun, but it's much better to trot up the mountain, smell the flowers and make things happen... it's good to take part.

- Every day brings something good, funny, new or exciting... jot it all down and remember to feel thankful.

- Know that sometimes you will make mistakes, after all you are only a unicorn. It's not the end of the world, so be kind to yourself.

- Your time is precious so spend it with like-minded unicorns and those who are important to you.

- Don't just chat, listen... there is wisdom all around if you choose to hear it.

- Make time to do nothing, and give your mind a good rest so you can be fresh as a daisy for whatever comes next.

- Cake is delicious but unicorns cannot live by cake alone... eat the kale too and you will keep healthy. And if you do some exercise as well that's even better.

- Buying and accumulating stuff will not make you happy, the best things in life really are free... hugs, kisses, sunshine, smiles, rainbows, flowers and small furry animals.

- Love yourself, even your lumps and bumps... they are all part of what makes you a unique, special and mythical creature.

Unicorn found that
unlikely friendships
could bring great joy.

Unicorn enjoyed
dressing for dinner;
today he was Morrissey,
but tomorrow he had big
plans for Frida Kahlo.

Unicorn thought it was better to look at the rainbow than to waste time digging for gold.

MASSIVE
POTS OF
GOLD HERE

He hadn't washed for
days but Unicorn still
smelled of roses.

Unicorn thought,
why walk when
you can skip.

Unicorn found
stroking the cat's ears
really therapeutic.

Unicorn had spent a bit too
long smelling the lavender.

Unicorn loved to feel
the rain on his cheeks.

Unicorn was feeling
thankful... he had
avoided the poop.

On a Wednesday,
Unicorn just
went around
complimenting
everyone.

YOUR SKIN
LOOKS RADIANT
TODAY

When stressed,
Unicorn put on loud
music and made a
warming casserole.

Someone had told
Unicorn that dark
chocolate was good
for his heart.

Unicorn tried really
hard not to judge a
book by its cover.

Being different could be hard, but Unicorn embraced it.

He had slept for
eight hours, and
Unicorn could
most definitely
smell the coffee.

Life had given Unicorn
lemons, so he decided to
squeeze them on his hair.

Unicorn found the
biggest challenge
with meditating was
clearing his mind of
happy thoughts.

Unicorn found his smile
was quite infectious.

Unicorn chose to
buy the shoes.

It might have been
a weed but Unicorn
thought it was
beautiful.

The upside of his roots showing was a trip to the salon for Friday fizz.

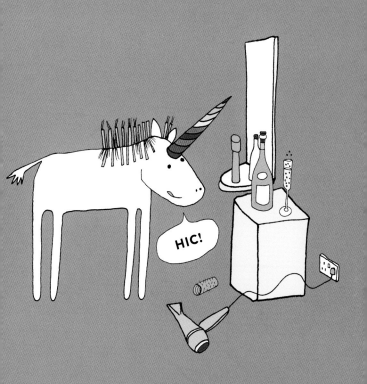

Being an ostrich
just didn't work
for Unicorn.

Unicorn enjoyed
the small things.

Unicorn decided to look at the bigger picture.

Unicorn laughed
so much at his own
joke that he made a
small puddle.

Today, Unicorn
wanted to make hay.

Unicorn had a
'can-do' attitude.

On bad days, Unicorn felt
sure that there would be
something better just
around the corner.

Unicorn danced like there
was no one looking.

Unicorn decided to wear the bikini.

With his shades on
Unicorn was feeling
invincible.

While concentrating
on his breathing
techniques, Unicorn
let out a small parp.

Unicorn enjoyed the wind in his hair.

Unicorn liked sharing, except
when it came to his potato chips.

Unicorn definitely
got his money's worth
out of his friends and
family deal.

Unicorn thought he
was good enough.

Unicorn's new exercise
class made him come alive.

Unicorn hoped you could never have too much love.

Unicorn decided it
was much better to
give than to receive.

On wet days, Unicorn
did his colouring.

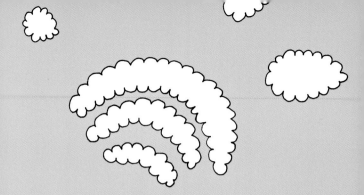

Watching clouds made
Unicorn feel really happy.

Unicorn chose to jump
in the puddles.

Unicorn found that
whenever one door shut,
another one opened.

The End... Now trot off
and be a unicorn.

An Hachette UK Company
www.hachette.co.uk

First published in Great Britain in
2017 by Spruce, a division of
Octopus Publishing Group Ltd
Carmelite House
50 Victoria Embankment
London EC4Y 0DZ

www.octopusbooks.co.uk
www.octopusbooksusa.com

Distributed in the US by
Hachette Book Group
1290 Avenue of the Americas
4th and 5th Floors
New York, NY 10104

Distributed in Canada by
Canadian Manda Group
664 Annette St.
Toronto, Ontario, Canada M6S 2C8

ISBN 978-1-84601-544-1

A CIP catalogue record for this
book is available from the British
Library.

Printed and bound in China.

18 17 16 15 14 13 12 11

Commissioning Editor
Sarah Ford

Editorial Assistant
Ellie Corbett

Designer and Illustrator
Anita Mangan

Senior Designer
Jaz Bahra

Production Controller
Sarah Kulasek-Boyd

Proofreader
Helen Ridge

CHARMING
SMALL HOTEL
GUIDES

FRANCE

& CORSICA

1993

CHARMING SMALL HOTEL GUIDES

FRANCE

& CORSICA

1993

Edited by Chris Gill

DUNCAN PETERSEN

Copyright   © Chris Gill 1993
               © Duncan Petersen Publishing Ltd 1993

This edition published 1993 by
Duncan Petersen Publishing Ltd,
54 Milson Road, London W14 0LB,
and distributed by
Automobile Association Publishing,
c/o Exel Logistics MS,
Invicta Warehouse, Sir Thomas Langley Road,
Medway City Estate, Rochester, Kent

Conceived, designed and produced by Duncan Petersen
Edited by Fox + Partners, The Old Forge,
Norton St Philip, Bath BA3 6LW

Editor Chris Gill
Assistant editors Julia Letts, Amanda Crook,
Nicola Cunningham, Nichola Atkins
Principal inspectors Ingrid Morgan, Martin Hitchcock
Proofreader Joshua Dubin
Art director Mel Petersen

A CIP catalogue record for this book is available from the
British Library

ISBN 1 872576 21 4

Typeset by Fox + Partners, Bath, and PCS Typesetting,
Frome
Originated by Reprocolor International S.R.I., Milan
Printed by G. Canale & C. SpA, Turin

Contents

Introduction	6
Reporting to the guides	9
Hotel location maps	10
North-west France	18
Île-de-France	43
North-east France	71
Western France	81
Eastern France	100
South-west France	126
Massif Central	156
South of France	168
Corsica	216
Readers' discounts	217
Index of hotel names	218
Index of hotel locations	221

★ Readers' discounts ★

Hotels in this guide picked out with stars, as in the heading above, have agreed to give our readers exclusive discounts on their normal rates. In total, these discounts are worth at least £250. There is a list of participating hotels, and more information about claiming the discounts, on page 217.

Introduction

This guide to French hotels – completely revised for 1993 – is part of a series also covering Italy, Spain, the British Isles, Germany and (this year) Austria.

The *Charming Small Hotel Guides* are different from other accommodation guides on the market. They are designed to satisfy what we believe to be the real needs of today's traveller – needs which have been served at best haphazardly by other guides. The most fundamental difference is suggested by the title: we aim to include only those hotels and guest-houses which are in some way captivating, and which are small enough to offer truly personal service, usually from the owner. In France, most of our recommendations have fewer than 20 rooms, and only a few have more than 30.

The guides are different in other ways, too. Our entries employ, above all, words: they contain not one symbol. They are written by people with something to say, not a bureaucracy which has long since lost the ability to distinguish the praiseworthy from the mediocre. The editorial team is small and highly experienced at assessing hotels, at noticing all-important details. Although we place great emphasis on consistency, we have made use of reports from members of the public, and would welcome more of them (see box following this introduction). Every entry, however brief, aims to give a coherent and definite feel of what it is actually like to stay in that place.

These are features which will reveal their worth only as you use your *Charming Small Hotel Guide*. Its other advantages are more obvious: it contains colour photographs of about one-third of the entries – usually the more attractive ones; the entries are presented in clear geographical groups; and each entry is categorized by the type of accommodation (for example, country inn).

Small French hotels
Small hotels have always had the special appeal that they can offer the traveller a personal welcome and personal attention. But small hotels in France have a special place in the hearts of travellers. Almost without exception, they are family-run, and have often been in the same family for generations. Many serve exceptionally good food. And, despite general inflation in France, their rooms remain generally affordable – particularly by British standards.

The establishments described in this guide are simply the 300 or so hotels, guest-houses, inns and bed-and-breakfast places that we believe most discriminating travellers would prefer to stay in, given the choice. We have left out some smart hotels on cost grounds. Even so, some undeniably pricey places are included. But there are plenty of places in this guide costing less than 400F a

Introduction

night for two.

Our ideal hotel has a peaceful, pretty setting; the building itself is either handsome or historic, or at least has a distinct character. The rooms are spacious, but on a human scale – not grand or intimidating. The decorations and furnishings are harmonious, comfortable and impeccably maintained, and include antique pieces that are meant to be used, not revered. The proprietors and staff are dedicated, thoughtful and sensitive in their pursuit of their guests' happiness – friendly and welcoming without being intrusive. Last but not least, the food, whether simple or ambitious, is fresh, interesting and carefully prepared. Elaborate facilities such as trouser-presses count for little, though we do generally list them.

Of course, not every hotel included here scores top marks on each of these counts. But it is surprising how many do respectably well on most fronts.

How to find an entry
In this guide, the entries are arranged by *département*, and theses are clustered in convenient regional groups. The regions, and within them the départements, are arranged in a sequence starting in the north-west and working southwards and eastwards. Corsica comes last.

To find a hotel in a particular area, simply browse through headings at the top of the pages until you find that area – or use the maps following this introduction to locate the appropriate pages. To locate a specific hotel or a hotel in a specific place, use the indexes at the back.

How to read an entry
At the top of each entry is a coloured bar highlighting the name of the town or village where the establishment is located, along with a categorization which gives some clue to its character.

Fact boxes
The fact box given for each hotel follows a standard pattern which requires little explanation; but:

Under **Tel** we give the telephone number, starting with (1) if the hotel is in the Paris area; if dialling such a number within Paris, you should omit the (1). When dialling Paris from the provinces, or vice versa, you must preface the whole number with 16. When dialling a provincial number in the provinces, the eight digits we give are all you need to dial. We now also give **Fax** numbers where appropriate.

Under **Location** we give information on the setting of the

Introduction

hotel and on its car parking arrangements, as well as pointers to help you find it.

Under **Food & drink** we list the meals available.

The basic **Prices** in this volume – unlike our volume on Britain and Ireland – are per **room**. We normally give the range of prices you can expect to pay for a room – from the cost of the cheapest single room in low season to the cost of the dearest double in high season. If the room price we give includes breakfast, we say so; otherwise, space permitting, we normally give the price of breakfast separately; where it is not given, allow 30F to 60F, according to the room price. We then give the prices of other meals, concentrating on fixed-price menus. If room-only or bed-and-breakfast terms are not available, we give either the price for dinner, bed and breakfast (DB&B), or for full board (FB) – all meals included. Prices includes tax and service.

Wherever possible we have given prices for 1993, but for many hotels these were not available when the guide was prepared. Bear in mind also that proprietors may change their prices from one year to another by much more than the rate of inflation. Always check before booking.

Under **Rooms** we summarize the number and style of bedrooms available. Our lists of facilities in bedrooms cover only mechanical gadgets, and not ornaments such as flowers or consumables such as toiletries or free drinks.

Under **Facilities** we list public rooms and then outdoor and sporting facilities which are immediately on hand; facilities in the vicinity of the hotel but not directly connected with it (for example, a nearby golf course) are not listed here, though they sometimes feature at the end of the main description in the **Nearby** section, which presents a selection of interesting things to see or do in the locality.

We use the following abbreviations for **Credit cards**:
    AE   American Express
    DC   Diners Club
    MC   MasterCard (Access/Eurocard)
    V   Visa (Barclaycard/Bank Americard/Carte Bleue etc)

The final entry in a fact box is normally the name of the proprietor(s); but where the hotel is run by a manager we give his or her name instead.

Reporting to the guides

Please write and tell us about your experiences of small hotels, guest-houses and inns, whether good or bad, whether listed in this edition or not. As well as hotels in France, we are interested in hotels in Britain and Ireland, Italy, Spain, Portugal, Austria, Switzerland, Germany and other European countries, and in the USA.

The address to write to is:

Chris Gill,
Editor,
Charming Small Hotel Guides,
The Old Forge,
Norton St Philip,
Bath, BA3 6LW,
England.

Checklist
Please use a separate sheet of paper for each report; include your name, address and telephone number on each report.

Your reports will be received with particular pleasure if they are typed, and if they are organized under the following headings:

Name of establishment
Town or village it is in, or nearest
Full address, including post code
Telephone number
Time and duration of visit
The building and setting
The public rooms
The bedrooms and bathrooms
Physical comfort (chairs, beds, heat, light, hot water)
Standards of maintenance and housekeeping
Atmosphere, welcome and service
Food
Value for money

We assume that in writing you have no objections to your views being published unpaid, either verbatim or in an edited version. Names of major outside contributors are acknowledged, at the editor's discretion, in the guide.

If you would be interested in looking at hotels on a professional basis on behalf of the guides, please include on a separate sheet a short CV and a summary of your travel and hotel-going experience.

Hotel location maps

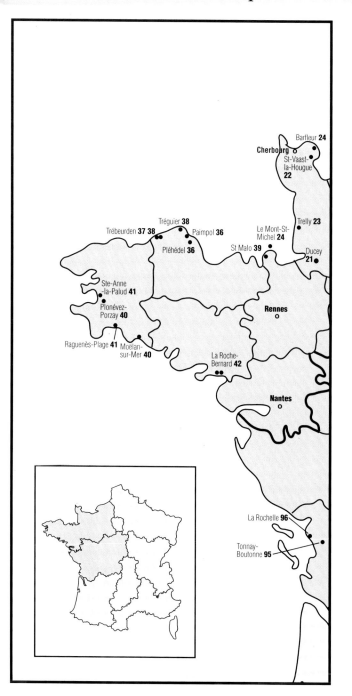

Barfleur **24**
Cherbourg
St-Vaast-la-Hougue **22**
Trelly **23**
Tréguier **38**
Paimpol **36**
Le Mont-St-Michel **24**
Trébeurden **37 38**
Pléhédel **36**
St Malo **39**
Ducey **21**
Ste-Anne-la-Palud **41**
Plonévez-Porzay **40**
Rennes
Raguenès-Plage **41** Moëlan-sur-Mer **40**
La Roche-Bernard **42**
Nantes
La Rochelle **96**
Tonnay-Boutonne **95**

Hotel location maps

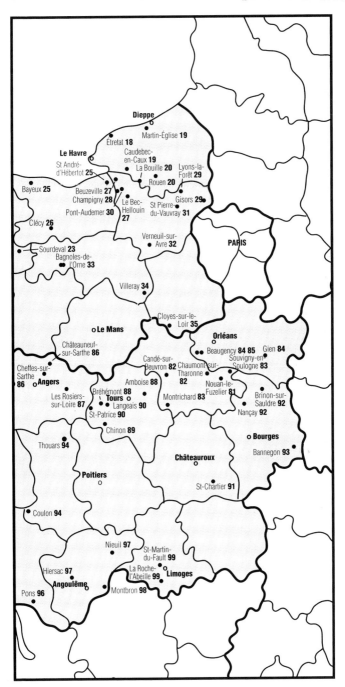

Dieppe

Martin-Église **19**

Étretat **18**
Caudebec-en-Caux **19**

Le Havre
St André-d'Hébertot **25**
La Bouille **20**
Lyons-la-Forêt **29**

Bayeux **25**
Beuzeville **27**
Champigny **28**
Rouen **20**
Le Bec-Helouin **27**
Pont-Audemer **30**
Gisors **29**
St Pierre-du-Vauvray **31**

Clécy **26**

Sourdeval **23**
Verneuil-sur-Avre **32**
PARIS

Bagnoles-de-l'Orne **33**

Villeray **34**

Le Mans
Cloyes-sur-le-Loir **35**

Châteauneuf-sur-Sarthe **86**
Orléans
Beaugency **84 85**
Gien **84**

Cheffes-sur-Sarthe **86**
Candé-sur-Beuvron **82**
Souvigny-en-Sologne **83**
Chaumont-sur-Tharonne **82**

Angers
Amboise **88**
Nouan-le-Fuzelier **81**

Les Rosiers-sur-Loire **87**
Bréhémont **88**
Tours
Langeais **90**
Montrichard **83**
Brinon-sur-Sauldre **92**

St-Patrice **90**
Nançay **92**

Chinon **89**

Thouars **94**
Bourges

Bannegon **93**

Châteauroux

Poitiers

St-Chartier **91**

Coulon **94**

Nieuil **97**
St-Martin-du-Fault **99**

Hiersac **97**
La Roche-l'Abeille **99**
Limoges

Pons **96**
Angoulême
Montbron **98**

11

Hotel location maps

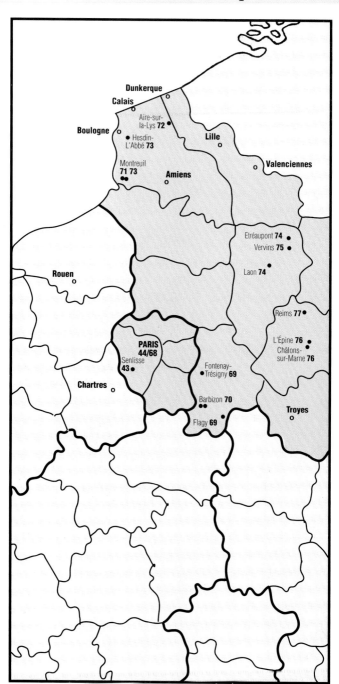

Hotel location maps

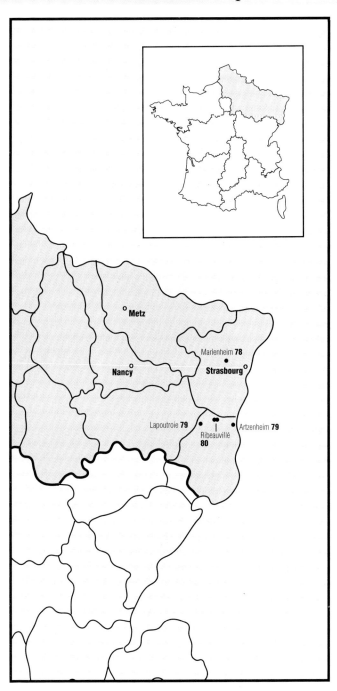

Metz

Marlenheim **78**

Nancy

Strasbourg

Lapoutroie **79**

Ribeauvillé
80

Artzenheim **79**

Hotel location maps

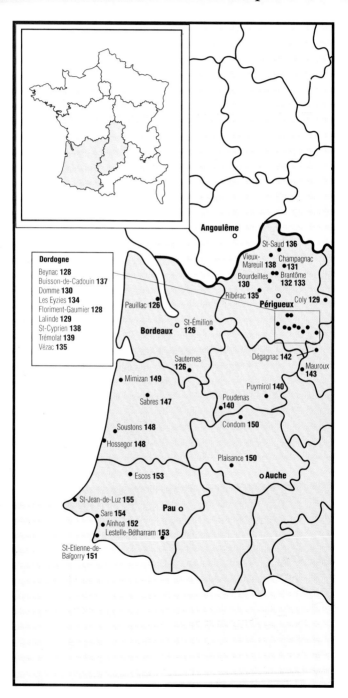

Dordogne
Beynac **128**
Buisson-de-Cadouin **137**
Domme **130**
Les Eyzies **134**
Floriment-Gaumier **128**
Lalinde **129**
St-Cyprien **138**
Trémolat **139**
Vézac **135**

Angoulême
○

St-Saud **136**
Vieux-
Mareuil **138** Champagnac
●**131**
Bourdeilles Brantôme
130 **132 133**
Ribérac **135**
Périgueux ○ Coly **129**

Pauillac **126**

St-Émilion
126

Bordeaux ○

Dégagnac **142**

Mauroux
143

Sauternes
126

Mimizan **149**

Puymirol **140**

Poudenas
140

Sabres **147**

Condom **150**

Soustons **148**
Hossegor **148**

Plaisance **150**

○ **Auche**

Escos **153**

St-Jean-de-Luz **155**
Sare **154**
Aïnhoa **152**
Lestelle-Bétharram **153**
St-Etienne-de-
Baïgorry **151**

Pau ○